MW01243285

psssst... that's you!

BEAUTIFUL DESIGNS FOR BEAUTIFUL PEOPLE

www.loveablefringe.com

Made in the USA
Middletown, DE
10 December 2022

17969659R00062